PRAYERS
and
SEVEN CONTEMPLATIONS
of the
SACRED MOTHER

Mary E. Kingsley

Published by WovenWord Press
811 Mapleton Ave.
Boulder, CO 80304
www.wovenword.com

Cover and book illustrations © 2004 by Lydia Ruyle
Cover and book design © 2004 by Vicki McVey
Author photo © 2004 by Keiko Guest

ISBN: 0971938350

DEDICATION

To my children, John Christian, Cameron, and Emma,
who light my path . . .

and to my husband Ted,
the most supportive life partner imaginable.

FOREWORD

This little book is a gift to anyone who would like to create a relationship with the Sacred Mother. I forged a relationship with her many years ago during a period of deep spiritual transition. At the time, I was in the inevitable place of needing to expand my image of the Divine to include the feminine as well as the masculine. And who would show up but Mary.

In much of Western Christian tradition Mary has been a powerful form of the Sacred Mother. Growing up Protestant, however, I had a kind of non-relationship with her. It was more or less limited to setting out the nativity scene. But in the midst of my journey to find a feminine dimension of the Divine, Mary came to me in a dream. She appeared as a weeping black woman, sitting on a porch of a quarantined slum. She wore an African headdress. A red one. And despite her sadness, she looked like she could straighten you out if necessary. As I passed her by, I recognized her true identity, and cried out to her: "I will come back for you." This is how I discovered that Mary was living impoverished and quarantined in my own soul.

As it turned out, I *did* go back for Mary. I began to explore her images and stories, particularly images of her as the Black Madonna. I was intrigued intellectually by how she is presently being reclaimed and re-visioned, by all the new feminist theological appropriations. And yet, what I most wanted was to find my own personal devotion to the Sacred Mother, to experience her in my heart. That is where the real mysteries, beauties and transformations in the spiritual life take place. I began to meditate on her, and it was not long before she had taken up residence not only in my heart, but within my creative life as well.

Through the beautiful prayers and contemplations in this book, we can experience the Sacred Mother in our *hearts*. Mary

Kingsley has given us a simple but powerful way of forging a real relationship with her. Not one merely thought about in our heads, but prayed in our hearts.

I am *still* "going back for Mary." In my dreams she no longer weeps.

Sue Monk Kidd

The Secret Life of Bees
The Dance of the Dissident Daughter

INTRODUCTION

This book is an expression of praise and adoration to the Sacred Feminine as she is manifested in the person of Mary, the Mother of Jesus Christ. Her appearance as the Holy Mother of the Christian tradition, a faith which has in large part shaped Western civilization, has provided throughout two millennia our only culturally sanctioned access to the ancient archetype of the Great Mother. As Mother of God, Mary holds an exclusive place in our collective psyche, as has the Goddess throughout thousands of years of human history. In recognizing her role as an image of the Divine Feminine in our culture, the message of Christ is not threatened or diminished in power, but emerges with fresh meaning and renewed energy for a world in desperate need.

The Mary of this book is a re-imagined Mary, who asks to be held in a new light. She asks us to consciously acknowledge the Sacred Feminine in our midst and to open ourselves to its deep healing. She wants us to wake up from the unconsciousness of a culture which for thousands of years has lived radically out of balance, and is therefore blind to its own abundance. This Mary calls us to recognize what we can accomplish within ourselves, to rediscover the power of compassion and inclusion, to recognize the sanctity of creation, to embrace the Mystery.

The historical Mary of the New Testament answers Divine guidance to initiate one of the most radical shifts in the story of humankind. She crosses the carefully drawn lines of her belief system and society to birth a new era.

The re-imagined Mary of these prayers is playing a similar role in our world today. She is asking us to look at the story of Jesus Christ in new ways, to look beyond the dictates of dogma in a passionate response to the message of unconditional love, forgiveness, and tolerance that Christ brought to the world two thousand years ago. She is telling us that Christ's incarnation, the Divine in matter, has implications for our relationships to the earth and to our own bodies that we have neglected to recognize in our faith traditions. The Divine is immanent not only in the person of Jesus, but in all life, all matter, all of Creation. God is ever present.

When we allow Mary as an expression of the Sacred Feminine, our concept of the Divine is made whole. As Mother of Christ she is Mother of all, Co-Creator of All That Is. God becomes Godde. To seek wholeness is the way of All Creation. Let us give Our Mother back to ourselves and be healed.

Note: Two words used in the text may be unfamiliar to you. These are *Godde*, which is a non gender designation for the Divine (source unknown), and *Namaste*, which is a Hindu greeting meaning "the Divine in me honors the Divine in you."

PRAYERS

Creed

I believe in a Divine Being,
Creator of the Universe,
who was made manifest in Jesus Christ,
born of the Divine union of Spirit and Matter as
expressed through the
Sacred Mother Mary.
He committed his life to truth,
lived, rejoiced, suffered, died
and returned to life,
in accordance
with the blessed cycles of all creation.

This Divine expression represents the
wholeness of existence,
the potential of all living things,
the coming together of Spirit and Matter,
of masculine and feminine,
the sacredness of nature,
the resurrection of life
and the integration of
Mind, Body and Spirit
that is the essence of
Godde the Creator.

Invocation

Our Mary, full of grace,
the Divine is within you
and surrounds you.
We see our own blessedness
reflected in you.
Godde waits in each of us
for the Divine expression
that is ours alone.
Gracious Mother,
be present with us
as we journey towards the Light
of our Sacred Destiny.
We pray for your guidance and protection
along the path.

Exaltation

Glory be to Godde,
the Mother, the Father
and the Divine Child.
As it has always been and always will be,
birth, life, death and rebirth,
the eternal cycle of creation.

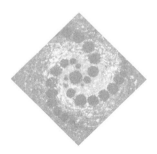

Our Mother

Sacred Mother,
You are all around us.
You are the matter of every living thing,
every plant, every animal, every rock.
You are the waters of every river,
the wind and rain,
the oceans, stars and sands of the shores.
You are the Divine body
that houses our spirit
and our Divine collective body,
the Earth.

Hallowed be thy name.
Sacred be thy flesh.

Let us be present to the gift of every moment and peacefully
relinquish ourselves to the higher good.

Heaven and Earth are one in you.
Through you our needs are met,
our wounds are healed
and our hearts
made whole.

Magnificence

My soul embraces the Divine
and my spirit rejoices
for I am worthy to receive the goodness of All Creation.
The blessings of abundance are mine to embrace.
I open my heart in Gratitude
for my Creator's Grace.

In Divine Love
there is no beginning or end,
no greater than or power over.
There is only Unity.
There is enough for each
and plenty for all.
All are deserving, for all are as one.
Magnificence

SEVEN CONTEMPLATIONS
of the
SACRED FEMININE

Meditations for a
New Consciousness

The Annunciation

Gratitude

Mary receives the message
that she has been
given the gift of the Divine Seed.
She says "yes" to the task of bringing Godde
to life.
The message of Christ is born into the world
through her act of co-creation with Godde.

Every moment we are given the opportunity
to manifest the Divine in our thoughts, actions,
and being.

May we be grateful.

The Visitation

Namaste

Mary's cousin Elizabeth
recognizes the Divine potential in Mary
and as she does so,
the life within her own belly is stirred.
We affirm Godde in each other
and awaken the Divine in ourselves.

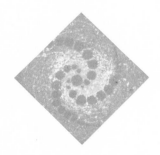

Namaste

The Mother's Joy

Release

The child is born.
The Now is born.
The waiting, the labor, the pain and the blood
are all forgotten in the glorious moment.
Everything that is, we have now.
Every moment we begin anew.

May we release and embrace
that which has been growing within.

The Mother's Sorrow

Faith

We confront in faith
the shadows of our world,
the shadows in ourselves,
the unthinkable:
lost potential, broken hopes and dreams,
sickness, suffering, death, war, hatred,
violence, abuse,
the darkness of a wounded world.

To venture wholeness is to embrace the shadows,
to seek the hidden face of the moon.

Healing our Body

Celebrating "Mater"

Mother, Mater, Matter
Sacred expression of the Feminine.
We seek the healing
of that which is broken or out of balance
in our bodies,
the disease or suffering that threatens
our wholeness.
We seek the healing of our Earth body
from the wounds inflicted by human ignorance
and greed.
We seek the healing of Our Mother
who brought us life,
who nurtures and sustains us.
If She is suffering so are we.
Our lives are one with Her.

Mother of the Christ,
Divine in Matter.

Healing World Soul

Anima Mundi

We seek the healing
of imbalances
that have been in place for thousands of years
and have created a way of being that is
destructive to life:
misuse of power, greed, dominance, oppression,
self-righteousness, fear, scarcity consciousness.
We recognize that at the center of our suffering
is the loss of the Feminine.
We hear the cries of the earth.
We seek the emergence of the Divine Mother,
Anima Mundi,
the Soul of the World.

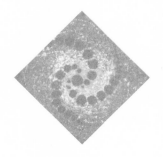

The Sacred Journey

Mary With Us

We pray for our individual needs and concerns.
We honor the Feminine,
our dreams and intuition, our inherent abilities to
nurture and to heal.
We honor the power of the unseen, of that
which is beyond.

We ask for guidance in seeking our own truth.
We seek the presence of the Divine,
the Mother and Father energies of Godde,
Creator of All That Is.

Amen

Afterword

This book was originally inspired by the Catholic Rosary. I am not a Catholic, nor have I ever been one. The small town of my childhood did have a Catholic Church, but I knew nothing of the reverence to the Holy Mother that took place there. I was raised in the Presbyterian Church right across the street, where Mary the Mother of Christ was little more than an image on Christmas cards, either riding on a donkey by the light of the star or kneeling in the stable gazing at the Christ Child.

I remember a Sunday School drawing of the boy Jesus working side-by-side with Joseph in his carpenter's shop, and another of him playing with other children. I wanted to see an image of him with his mother, to be reminded that he had one. Her absence gave me vague feelings of sorrow and anxiety that I couldn't articulate, yet there was an awareness that the picture was less than complete.

As a young adult I joined another mainstream church, drawn in by what I perceived to be a bit more theological elbow room than other denominations. By then I had come to question the male dominated structure of the Church, but as yet had not come up against anything that I couldn't reconcile within myself. Then there was an incident in an adult Sunday School class, which happened that day to be led by a clergyman. He made the comment that the Catholic Church overemphasizes the role of Mary the Mother of Christ and takes too much of the focus away from Jesus.

I raised my hand. I offered the possibility that perhaps they were onto something quite valuable, that Mary represents something we have ignored—the feminine, motherly aspect of the Divine. After all, she is the Mother of God. He replied emphatically that I was on the wrong track. "Mary is nothing!" he exclaimed. My heart said otherwise. At that moment I knew deeply that I had somehow embarked on a new path, that I was beginning my own journey.

It has been several years since I began my exploration of the Sacred Feminine and all of its implications for our selves, our culture and our planet. I have experienced her in many aspects: in nature, in the earth itself, in my growing awareness of my self and my body. These have been years of building a marriage, of having babies, of losing pregnancies, of raising children, of seeking, questioning, multi-tasking, of trying to do a decent job in an imperfect world, of holding on to faith that there is something bigger than all of us out there and that not only is it good, but that it will ultimately prevail. These have been years in which few things are certain, yet there is one thing that is to me as certain as the sunrise. As a world, we are in great need of our Mother.

One of my yoga teachers once shared this poignant anecdote in class. He said that when he was a child, he never felt secure when his mother was gone. "But when Mother was home," he said, "I was free to play and explore."

Although to some extent Mary has been allowed to serve that purpose in the Catholic Church, as a larger culture our Mother is not home. Yet it is not She who has abandoned us. We have excluded Her to our profound detriment, seeking our wholeness in static institutions, addictions, and the excesses that are inherent in our society. We must allow Her back into our consciousness if we are to recover from the wounds we have inflicted on ourselves and on the planet.

The Sacred Feminine has been with us since the beginning of time. She comes to us throughout history with many names and faces, each given to Her as a reflection of the times and people who acknowledged her. She is known as Isis of Egypt, Cybele of Turkey, Pachamama of Peru, Brigid of Ireland, Sophia, Mater Terra, Kali, Tara, and many, many more throughout time and the world. For the ancients, she was all-powerful, the Goddess of fertility, birth-giver, a reflection not only of the human female but of nature and the earth itself, central in her role as the source of all life.

Western history, however, reveals a shift in the perception of the feminine in society. In the myths of ancient Greece, woman loses even her exclusive role as child bearer when Athena springs from the head of her father Zeus. As history progresses and the story of the Israelites leads into the beginnings of Christianity, the many Gods of our ancestors are replaced by one male God. In time, the Great Mother is rejected as antithetical to the power and goodness of the Father God, as is woman, her human counterpart, who often bears the legacy of Eve as the single cause of suffering for all of humankind.

So it is through Mary the Mother of Christ that the Sacred Feminine finds her way into our culture at all. She has prevailed, yet only to the extent that she can be expressed within the confines of Church doctrine. It was through my own experience in seeking a personal relationship with her that I came to the awareness of another Mary–a more complete Mary for our times. It is in response to this Mary that I wrote these prayers.

About a year and a half ago, during a particularly stressful time with my teenage children, I began to feel a deep longing for communion with the Feminine Divine in her manifestation as the Mother of Jesus. I was taken back to that void in my childhood understanding of Christ's life. What was Jesus like as a teenager and how did Mary, his earthly mother, handle a boy who she'd been told was God? What were her days like? I wanted to talk to her, to be with her, to have her companionship as I went through this phase of my life.

I thought that learning the Catholic Rosary would be the answer. A friend showed me how to do it and even gave me my first beads. I thanked her, took them home with the best of intentions, and began to pray. I tried it several times and felt discouraged.

Where was the Mary who was calling me into communion–the spirited woman who in her time ushered in a new era for all of humanity? Even in the prayers designed for her adoration, even in her glory, she is still portrayed as subservient to the higher male powers–the Father and the Son. The language is so pointedly designed to keep her subordinate, to limit her power, as to imply the threat that she poses if allowed full expression. The Patriarchal overlay weighs heavily and is impossible to ignore.

Traditionally, Mary is allowed only the traits befitting a Church dogma that essentially rejects the Sacred Feminine. Doctrine has erased her sexuality, for the human body and its relationship to the rhythms of earth and nature are too closely associated with the Goddess. She has long been our model for immense love, tenderness and nurturing, qualities which resonate throughout humanity. Yet in addition, great emphasis is placed on her perfect obedience, her unwavering servitude, her subservience to a religious hierarchy.

Our human hearts tell us there is much more to her than that. Where can we experience and acknowledge her fierceness, her independent spirit and her courage?

I needed a way to pray to Mary the woman and Mother of All as I perceived her, so I thought I'd write my own Rosary. At first I tried to use the existing structure and just change words here and there, but what I discovered was something else that wanted to be written. I feel that *Prayers and Seven Contemplations of the Sacred Feminine* was waiting to be expressed, and somehow I provided an opening at the right moment in time.

I wrote the prayers for my own use in accordance with a personal theology, but I did share them with a spiritual mentor at Cedar Hill Enrichment Center in Georgia. Her reaction was that they needed to be shared further, and she asked me to present them at the dedication of an outdoor chapel at Cedar Hill on August 15th, the Feast of the Assumption of Mary, 2002.

The prayers were received with immense gratitude and enthusiasm. Many people wanted copies, and wanted them for others. Within a few weeks of this event, with the help and support of friends and family, we had put together literally hundreds of booklets and continued to receive numerous requests. It seemed that whatever voice had come through in these prayers and meditations spoke not only to me but to others as well.

I am grateful for the opportunity to share this work more widely. My hope is that it reaches all who are searching for the new Mary, whether they know it or not.

A Word About Creeds

What is a creed? It is a statement of belief which we use to outline the principles of our institutions, our religions in particular. Many of us grew up memorizing the creeds that told us what we were to believe and, as in my case, reciting them with a feeling of pride and righteousness. I felt a great accomplishment in knowing the Apostle's Creed and later on the Nicene Creed by heart.

Yet as I grew older and began learning to own the truth of my own journey, the unchanging nature of the old creeds began to feel less and less like they reflected my spiritual path. I could no longer stand in church and recite the centuries old codes without wanting to leave out certain words or lines and add others. I am taught that the words of the Apostle's and the Nicene Creeds are the cornerstone of Christian church doctrine. If that is so, then it would seem that I must be able to make these statements authentically if I am to call myself a Christian.

Is this then the definition of a Christian, to be able to recite with conviction words that were written hundreds of years after the life of Christ, in a radically changed social environment from that in which he lived and taught? Is it that I must believe the creed as stated before I can be joined with the one Divine Mind in the next life?

The creeds are statements of a belief system handed down by architects of a human institution with profound historical and political implications. Yet as I have come to know the Sacred Feminine, I have found myself seeking a wider understanding of Christ's message to the world. One has only to look around at the vast diversity of our universe and question the thinking that demands we all experience Divine Love in the same manner. Martin Buber once stated "God made so many different kinds of people, why would he allow only one way . . .?"

If this is so, then why have a Creed? Is it to define our beliefs so that we may create a sense of security and belonging? When we make a statement of collective belief intended to define and guide, what we create is a structure that some will fit into and others will not. Those within the structure may agree that this is the point, that it is the free will of every human to decide whether or not they accept the terms and therefore gain access to God. Yet given this gift of the infinite diversity of creation, how can there be one structure or institution that embraces all that is God and all truth for all beings for all time?

When a community or society locks into a statement of belief and assumes its unchanged constancy for thousands of years, there is inevitably a growing conflict between the statement itself and the evolving, spirit-filled human experience of God. We attempt to create Truth with words, but words can become Dogma and Truth is immense, beyond written language, beyond human experience and understanding.

Albert Schweitzer is credited with saying, "Dogma divides, Spirit unites." So if a creed is even necessary or desirable, as are channel markers through the narrow passages of our lives, then is there a way to express belief without creating dogma around it?

I look to nature for the answers, for it is in our own nature and the world around us that we witness the Divine, the gift of manifestation that Jesus represents. In this experience, I see only two things as constant. The first is the omnipresence of God, and the second is, ironically, a permanent state of change. So as things are constantly changing, growing, evolving, God is ever present yet ever revealed anew.

Is there a statement of belief that could reflect this oxymoron of constancy and change? If so, it would have to be the ideological counterpart to the holograph and offer a multitude of light, angles and reflections to be true to the spiritual needs of this human path. It would not look the same to everyone who saw it and as one held it, it would shift and change. As one looks at the holograph, new colors and images are always emerging, new ways of seeing it are always revealed.

I cannot profess to know how to express such a thing with the written word. Therefore I offer the best that I know how, and that is simply an honest statement of what I believe to be truth at this moment in my journey. I don't think it is the Only Truth, nor do I think it is All That Is True. It is merely a facet of the vast reality that is beyond our human knowing.

And so while offering you a Creed in this small book of prayers, I also offer to you from the depths of my being a heart that is open to you and your creed, whoever you are and whatever you believe, and wherever it is that your journey is taking you. Whatever your path, you are surrounded by God because you cannot help but be surrounded by God. By listening and living from your own Truth you are reflecting God in all you do, which is, I believe, the Divine purpose of all living things.

Seven Questions

On the following pages I invite you to explore your own experience of the Sacred Feminine. You may want to write down any dreams, thoughts or prayers that come as you begin this process. Consider the questions as starting points and see where each one leads, being open to the rich discoveries that will surely follow.

Mary E. Kingsley

How does an awareness of the Feminine Divine affect your life
and your perceptions of the world around you?

Notes

Mary E. Kingsley

How do you see Mary, the Mother of Jesus as an expression of
the Feminine aspect of God?

Notes

How do you see the world changing if the Sacred Feminine is allowed back into our cultural consciousness?

Notes

Mary E. Kingsley

When God becomes Godde, how does that feel to you?

Notes

As Mary the Mother of Jesus was called to manifest the Divine into the world, how is it that you are being called to co-create with Godde? What seed or gift within you is waiting to be expressed?

Notes

How can an awareness of the Sacred Feminine affect your relationships with others and your self?

Notes

Mary E. Kingsley

What is your Creed at this point in your spiritual journey?

Notes

To order:
WovenWord Press
811 Mapleton Ave.
Boulder, CO 80304
toll free Phone: 888 773 7738
email: books@wovenword.com
web: www.wovenword.com

Contact and workshop information;
Contemplations7@aol.com